MW01199019

LOOKING
GLASS

A Man's Reflections Within the Scope of Dating & Relationships

Vernon V. Jackson Jr.

The Looking Glass
A Man's Reflections Within the Scope of Dating &
Relationships

Vernon V. Jackson Jr.

Copyright © 2019 by
Vernon V. Jackson Jr. & Beyond Words Publishing

ISBN: 978-0-578-59632-7

TABLE OF CONTENTS

INTRODUCTION

In my adult life, I've dated under the weight of expectations, established by society, my community, the women I've dated, etc. Until, one day, I let all the expectations go. I took time to experience dating and living from an observer's perspective.

I learned how to listen. Ask questions. But more importantly, out of this space came ownership of Self.

The parallel: building a relationship with Self is in principle the same as building relationships with others.

The lessons learned and contemplated out of this time, birthed the ideas you're holding in your hand, gathered and aptly titled, *Looking Glass*.

I wrote this book to offer some transparency for the women looking to understand and the men looking to articulate. Ideally, I wanted to give women insight and a window into what a guy, like myself, thinks and thought about dating and relationships from a place of deep reflection and love. Not from a place driven by fear, false perceptions, and hyper-masculinity.

I wanted to address how the dating landscape has changed drastically and how we haven't evolved in our systems of dating and communication to move in it freely. In all, I want the sharing of my perspective to challenge you to listen and ask questions differently. Begin to ask questions in order to understand, not only the other person but also yourself.

Challenge yourself to find out where your heart is. Where and how do you need to grow so you can offer your fully realized Self to the process of dating and relationships? It's important to know what you're truly bringing to the relationships you desire to build.

Use this book as a conversation starter. Talk with friends of the same or opposite sex to uncover the answers and enjoy the depth of different points of view. Ask yourself some questions in the process.

"How and why have I been dating?"

"Has it worked?"

"What do I really know about myself?"

"Why haven't I asked and answered certain questions for myself before?"

"What do I have the capacity for? Dating or marriage?"

This isn't about either side being right or wrong. I offer "Reflections" for every piece because it's important for me to stress the fact that both men and women go through many of the same things but in different ways. It's important to make room to share our different experiences with each other openly. All our experiences are valid. The goal is to develop common empathy.

Everyone has a heart story. It's important for you to discover your own before you can have the capacity to receive the person who's willing to read it.

Understand that this is a process. It takes work. However, if you do it right, it can also be fun!

A healthy relationship with Self equals healthy relationships with others.

Let's begin.

Understanding a Man's Heart Story.

If women really want to understand
why a man is where he is emotionally,
she should ask him about his heart story.
Not to use it against him but to understand him!

•••

Men Have Feelings

As men we don't let our feelings
and heart in too many times.

My perspective as a man is
when it comes to the disappointment
and challenges of dating
we experience them first.

As a result, we've learned how to build and live with our
protective blocks.

...

Note to the Fellas
Fellas we must learn how to acknowledge and express our
feelings while also being open to reason thereafter. It's
okay to be honest about getting tired of experiencing
disappointments. Everyone has looked for love in the
wrong places and in the wrong ways. However, it's not
okay that we operate from a place of hurt and decide to
give up entirely or continue to live in any dysfunction.

Note to the Ladies
Being open to a man expressing his feelings, whether or
not you agree with him, is important. Having the posture
that allows him to do this from a place of love is
paramount in understanding him. Especially if he's a man

that never had the space to be vulnerable and honest in his relationships.

Reflections
Providing a space for a man to express his feelings may bridge disconnected places in relationships. Some men take getting "shot down" differently than others, just like women.

Women stop dating once someone has hurt them too many times and are lied to on the regular. So do, men. The problem is we don't talk about it with each other.

The understanding we want takes real dialogue. We can't continue to just move forward without understanding who we are.

Cry like a man.

•••

The Approach

Whether or not we want to believe it, men have feelings
too.

Approaching the woman
he wants with respect
and tenderness
too many times
only to be met with a stank face or attitude,
too many times
would make some men more calculated
on who they approach.

Men have been taking hits since we first started taking
our crush homemade valentine cards and have dealt with
disappointing outcomes since then.

Developing calluses on our hearts and minds just happens.

•••

Note to the Fellas
Every woman of the Now is not the woman of yesterday.
Find the balance in the pursuit and the reality of potential
failure as a reflection of what doesn't fit you, rather than
see yourself as being the problem. Unless you have
certain characteristics you know are actual problems. If
you want a relationship or desire to marry, you won't get
through the dating process unscathed. But you can get out

of the process emotionally intact if you accept that it's all a part of the process.

Note to the Ladies

In relationships don't expect men to be robots or emotionless creatures. Don't expect us to pretend like nothing can hurt us, including our past, or like we can't have feelings. Women should allow men to acknowledge our hurt too.

Reflections: Getting turned downed repeatedly is draining. Sometimes the man you want to want you may just need a little encouragement or an assist. Yes, it's old school and customary for the man to approach you. However, some men need to know they have the green light first before they make the approach. You can do this with a simple hello. Use any tool that will be a conversation starter.

Adapt

Men are met with disappointment and havoc before a woman ever has to. Because we are the first ones to make the approach at the beginning when the attraction happens.

We are the ones who go out and express our feelings before the woman ever does.

So, we're conditioned to develop calluses in order to withstand the dating process. This way we don't get manipulated as much by emotions.

We have a head start on choosing logic in the dating process. We develop categories and move forward logically.

•••

Reflections
Men learn how to move in relationships more logically than women. Either from too much emotional hurt or we've learned from the hurt of other men. The ability for some of us to feel again or trust is a process. We all have our stories it's just that everyone moves from theirs differently.

Don't focus on how you think a man should be vs. acknowledging how your man actually is!

•••

Emotional Survival

The pressure to be the men
we were never taught to be
the best way we can
only to find that our best
was or is not enough.

On the flip side there are women who have put their trust
in men
only to have those men lead them to a dead end.
Left with picking up the pieces
they try to create someone new
out of themselves.

Surviving the gauntlet
of a male-dominated world
where "some" men verbally abused them
they create or are forced to develop both mental and
emotional calluses.
Once formed, calluses are the same for men and women.
We just express our calluses differently.

•••

Reflections
We can't control what life gives us or how things happen.
We can control what we make of ourselves and the
identity we accept for ourselves. Use your calluses to
protect you, but don't develop them so much that you're
no longer able to feel what's genuine!

Your story can and will heal the you that didn't have you
to speak up for and to you!

•••

Love Isn't Manufactured

I was never groomed for
the image of what it looked like
to project all that you were taught to look for.

To love
in a way
that I wasn't able to emulate
through my lifestyle
So, I...
in my struggle
struggled, to match
my ideal with your ideal with the reality
of what I could provide
to match yours and mines,
expectations that are needed in a marriage.

A relationship
but based on the projections
of our true foundation the image became blurry
pixilated
incomplete.

I didn't match what you were groomed to receive
and you didn't have the grace to complete me or teach me.

It's hard
playing the part of a character
when you weren't schooled on the backstory

not knowing the character of the character.

How would you feel
to be fired from a job
that just didn't want to teach you
the position?
Even worse,
they couldn't teach you the position
because they didn't understand the role
they wanted you in.
So, the role they didn't want you in.

Maybe we both in real life
were victims of ignorance
walking on the path
that was good and beautiful
from a distance.

•••

Reflections
The characteristics we love in a person don't just happen.
They're groomed. Chosen. Learned over time.

Having expectations of what the other person is supposed
to do to suit us and to make us complete, sets us up for
failure and ultimately gives the relationship an unleveled
foundation.

As adult men and women, having expectations and
knowing what we want is not enough.

Learning the story of our partners while also unselfishly sharing our own, in order to offer insight for a deeper understanding, is a must. They're not to be shared with just anyone, but the potential ones.

The Veil

As much as I find marriage beautiful
and want to believe in it...

Believe me
a long term, intimate relationship
fills my heart
but where do I start?

Me, like a lot of men
weren't groomed to be husbands
not to mention the marriages
a lot of us witness
start in the church
but found
ended by a judge's decision.

So, we quantify
the time we spent
money we spent
expectations met with disappointment.

I'd love to be vulnerable and open
but too many women walk around
with hearts that are hurt and full
with no place for love to pour into.

I've seen too many women cheating
and too many men doing the same thing.

Why would I put myself in a place
to potentially go through the same thing?

I'm confused by it all.

Relationships are a crap shoot
and I'm no gambler
I'd love to love her
but at what cost?

•••

Reflections
We groom guys to put it all out on the table in the
beginning stages. Time. Money. Feelings. After a while
you hear stories of other relationships. The facts and
perspectives of how they end. Then we ask ourselves the
questions:

"What am I doing this for?
Am I doing it for emotional connection, a relationship, or
business? What is my why?"

There's a difference between what marriage is and how
we look at it. We base these things on how people treat
marriage, the experiences we witness, and the heartbreak
we suffer. We have to ask ourselves what are we in this
for? And if it goes left, what are you willing to lose?

Creating a safe space, while being consistent and making
a space for someone in that space, to be honest about the

space they're in, may create an opportunity for them to move past their own reserves about marriage and long-term commitment.

Regardless of your idea of what a man is... realize many
men have been broken just like you.

•••

KNOWING YOURSELF BEFORE DATING INTENTIONALLY.

I'm okay with having an opinion with no need for other's validation.

•••

Responsible for My Space My Energy

As a person...
- I've learned at principle what my vibe is and what my community needs are.
- I don't force myself to be around people.
- I don't trust feelings even though I allow myself to feel.
- The way I see feelings has altered me a lot. I've become emotionally neutral.

As a father to be, I now know the kind of father I want to be. The one my future child needs me to be.

As a husband to be, I now know the kind of husband I want to be. The one *she* needs and can receive and not who I want her to have.

•••

Reflections
The more that I've gotten to the depth of who I actually am and what I want, the less mess I have in my space. There are trillions of sounds that don't make it into my song. Everything and everyone doesn't fit.

In relationships I began asking myself, "What's more important, being the person I want to be or being who they need me to be? Which comes first?"

The only time truth and facts should stop you from growth is when you aren't able to receive them.

We do a poor job in the acknowledgment of each other's stories and treat each other like servants rather than partners.

•••

Stand or Fall

I fall in love regularly
but I stand in love rarely.

•••

Reflections
Falling in love is frequent because I allow myself to be attracted to who I'm attracted to. We often have something that just makes us click.

But standing in love is different. Standing in love means continually choosing. Especially when it's at a cost to ourselves. It's rare because everyone doesn't want that with you or isn't fit for it.

The Value in Solitude

Being single has taught me
to appreciate the gift of connection,
fully,
and how rare it is,
to work at it,
and compromise for it,
like I compromise or adjust for my goals and business.
Singleness has taught me not to have unrealistic
expectations.

The perspective I've lived from in this space has been to
be present in it,
to observe how people are when it comes to how I allow
myself to be.
To truly see how they respond to me.

Authentic, mutual, connection in whatever capacity is
rare. It's rare. Knowing I value it, I now treat it differently.

•••

Reflections
Men and woman make compromises and will figure out
more problems and work harder in everything else other
than their relationships.

Learn Your Instrument

Rhythm.
If you know your sound
and tune
you know how to make music
with anyone who knows
their own instrument.

•••

Reflections
Developing self-awareness is essentially the fine tuning of
our instruments. This is what makes us unique.

A musician that understands their instrument understands
its stress points. The do's and don'ts and respects those
boundaries. We must do the same for ourselves and each
other.

Every musician doesn't make it into the band if they don't
fit. Accepting your sound makes it easier to know where
you fit and where you don't.

It's okay to be happy
beyond the reality of other people.
Their happiness is none of your business and your
happiness is none of theirs.
Let them argue with themselves.

•••

Adapt | Adjust | Grow

As men and women, we have to become more conscious of how the landscape and environment of relationships is changing.

The perception of what the roles are for men and women are being challenged, refined, and amended but no one knows what the amendments are.

We go our whole lives discovering who we are and how we operate while still being challenged at times even with what we come up with to stand for.

We date with the underlying expectation
that the other person should know their role or the role to play in our lives.

We literally date with the mindset of, "So what can you do for me?" Rather than "what can I do for the nurturing of the union we're trying to cultivate." No matter what it is.

As we learn to survive the single process, we must also know that the person we've become while being single needs to compromise things to make their relationships cohesive.

•••

Reflections

We do not manufacture relationship characteristics. They are groomed and coached. Whether by you or the person before you.

Grooming and coaching someone for you in your language takes time. You did not mature overnight, and neither will your relationships.

You have to grow roots before you grow up!

•••

Exposed Roots

In this one life I've been given
the grace to live in,
I've found myself
in times that've been recent
finding myself,
diving in and out
of experiences
just trying to feel
something different.

Hoping the hope that I put into it
would yield something different,
hopefully show me
something different.

However, on the search
I found that the more that I found
something outside of me
the more I was running
from what I needed to see
inside of me.

I wasn't allowing myself
to see,
to see it,
the real elephant in the room.

I was running, walking, turning a blind eye to me

to what I'd become
and what I was running from.

I have been selfish,
selfish from me to me
holding myself
and hiding myself from me
not being honest with myself
about how I really feel about...me!

So, I was pulling the wool over my own eyes.

See I, did not want to see
that I was the reason
I felt disconnected
to the universe
in the ways that made me feel so alive,
I too had done things
that cost trust
the same way that
they stole trust from me.

It was like history repeating itself
but I just wanted to be the victim,
I didn't trust myself to go deeper
to accept the challenges.

So, I paused to understand
what the value meant to be challenged,
to really focus on that responsibility.

Then I accepted
that a risk is still a risk
no matter how calculated.

However, doing too much calculating
had me sitting still
but honestly I needed
to listen and to heal.

We can't rush life
and no matter how much we get
there is still something different
to reach for
to dig for
to dust off
to be uncomfortable with or about
so, you insert challenge
because as long as there is a challenge
there lies another chance to grow
to experience life
through the invitation of that challenge.

God is in the invitation
because in reality
a challenge is really an invitation
or an opportunity to take a journey into you.

No matter how far challenge takes you
on the outside
sometimes the hardest thing to do
is to face others

but the life change happens
when we face ourselves.

To risk it all on not just anything, but everything!

Life is a journey, a process
and it takes time.

God is in time
thankfully, because healing takes time
but growth, growth takes action!

We must be action
and while we are still above ground
on this earth
our responsibility rather in stillness
or in movement
is to GO!

•••

Reflections
Being honest with myself is the hardest thing I've had to
do.
Facing how and where I've created my own mess. To
connect to the outside world in simpler forms means we
have to know what's going on within us.

Whether we do it through art or do it through therapy, we
need to do a heart check and know our spirit placement.

Origin is Everything

What are you positioned for?

What have you created the capacity to receive?
A business partner? A lover? A friend? A marriage? A
situationship?

Because it isn't about what you "want" because if that
were the case you and everyone else would have it.

You can only receive what you have the space for. If you
want a relationship but you're still healing and learning
who you are, then you probably only have the capacity for
a friendship.

•••

Reflections
Being honest with ourselves about what we have the
emotional capacity for is highly important when it comes
to dating. Wanting something and having the capacity for
it is different.

For instance, if you want to be married but really only
have the communication and listening capacity for short-
term dating you're setting yourself up for failure. You
need the proper tools to handle marriage and they differ
from the ones you use while dating.

Receiving things before we have the capacity for them sets us up to be disappointed, unfulfilled, and angry. Run your own race.

Be mindful about bringing the residue from past situationships to your current relationships.

•••

DATING: THE RULES HAVE CHANGED.

Don't place long-term standards and expectations on short-term situations.

•••

Dating Categories

There are categories in dating.

Be able to differentiate between the level of attraction you have for someone and then categorize it.

For instance, if you like someone from just a physical standpoint, but don't feel a "connection" to them, then it's just sexual. Do not emotionally put them into the relationship category.

You must define what these categories look like for you. You must know what you should let in and what not to let into your heart. Be able to articulate where you are with that person. AND DO IT!

Do not try to put or have expectations of someone in the friendship or sexual attraction category with the criteria of someone in the relationship category.

•••

Reflections
We must create the definitions for the categories to give ourselves context. To develop a process that checks and balances our feelings and logic.

When you realize and accept that you are not for
everyone and everyone is not for you and
FOR YOU!
Life gets a lot more weightless!

•••

Boxes | Connection | Checklists

Do people really fall in love with the boxes they check?
It feels like the boxes they check aren't the person you
are.

Personally, I can't like you, if I don't like you.
Love, a relationship, companionship
or any other ship
that takes time and intentionality
to build
before you can take it on the waters
to sail on to.

I can't like or love someone
I don't feel connected to, or don't feel a vibe that says, "I
don't want to be without you," or "I'm filled by doing life
with you."

A vibe,
a rhythm that's reciprocal
not by balance
but by rhythm.

In rhythm
I've matured a little
so, I don't really love the same
I don't spit game
maybe it's because of the many conversations,

the logical, emotional exchanges of conversation with
God's beautiful creation
that confessed and professed
that all they wanted was upfront honesty
with a hint of vulnerability.

But honestly,
honestly as much as honesty has gotten me a mind that's
free, it's pushed more people away.

As if I missed the real hint,
"It's like: I like honesty but not that honest."
Like the indirect admittance
that a little finesse and game is what's needed.
But to me when the matters of the heart
matter, I should play no games.

All intentions
should be laid,
no confusion
and no assumptions could be made.

Sexes don't like to be grouped together,
stereotyped,
but when at principle
a lot of the woman have been alike,
then how do you not adapt
and see that a lot of woman are alike.

Dating when you know yourself is
way more difficult than when you don't,

but I'd rather know what I stand for
and who and why
then to stand with someone
who didn't know me but just checked me off a box and
wanted a wedding and a ring.

Spend more time impressing Instagram
than impressing me
rather get dressed for the gram
than to get dressed for me.

I want someone
who wants a marriage and me!
who stands by what they say
and when they don't,
don't blame me!

But the reality is
sometimes a connection is instant
but the functionality takes time,
intention, vulnerability,
and courageous conversation.

No matter what angle,
time is still the most important ingredient.

Because God is in time
so, we can't rush it.
So, no matter the angle just communicate...and be patient.

•••

Reflections

Everyone has an angle they tie their connection to. Some people take their time while others don't need time.

No matter what, if the person you want is worth having, do what's necessary. Be what's needed. Let time do what only time can do.

Being angry that someone doesn't see you how you want them to, when you want them to, is entitlement.

Some of us fall in love when our lists are met and others when the connection is. Dating is complicated because we make it complicated.

We don't want to be wrong or hurt. We want what we want from who we want it from and tolerate people that don't fit fully.

Established grounds of communication are essential and if the people we're interested in don't see this, should we really work hard to convince them?

What's Projected Isn't Always Received

Intimidation vs. not being approachable. I feel that many women have this "because I'm successful, I intimidate men" mindset.

When maybe it's more that a man may feel that she is unapproachable.

If we don't know you, how do we know you're successful or smart?

What we do know is how you come off. We don't have a device that we can hold up or an app that says, "yep, she's approachable."

We [men] are not [easily] intimidated. We just don't want to approach a woman who we think is projecting her unwillingness to have a conversation and may just take our nice/gentle approach and throw it back in our faces.

The make believe or real success does not scare us. The 'I'm cool' vibe deters us.

Most of us men don't care to argue to convince a woman to talk to them.

How does a man know that a woman is successful if he doesn't know her?
If he just met her at hello?

The attitude she exudes may project her to be unapproachable or not easily reachable. But that comes with a cost.

Being unapproachable is different.

•••

Note to the Ladies
A guy may be intimidated, but it doesn't make him weak, it makes him human.

Reflections
We all project something we want other people to receive about us. It doesn't mean they will.

We all uniquely have a certain language or dialect that everyone doesn't speak. Except the ones that do.

For some men we show we want to talk to a woman or show we're attracted to a woman by approaching her. The women that either invites us to talk or buys us a drink or smiles in our direction are the ones that match what we are giving off. Sometimes we approach a woman that doesn't give that signal just to try to most times it ends up being a bad decision.

So, it's not always about being intimidated. Being unapproachable is more about the signal than it is about a woman being successful.

Some men pay money just so you can pay us some attention.

•••

The New Independence

How do you want to be independent
but dependent,
how is that?

You want to have your own money
but you want me to spend mine
on you without even knowing
rather you actually know me,
or like me, or want me,
you've lost me.

There is a group of us men that get overlooked.

We don't play with love to get to sex,
we don't withhold truth to get to what's next,
we don't assume what is and what isn't,
we take it for what it is and what it isn't,
no lies, no gimmicks.

It's like some women want to be a woman
when it's beneficial to them,
want the old treatment
but don't have the old school tools to
reciprocate the things they demand us to do.

There is a new school woman and a new school man too.

We want a woman

to know what she wants
as much as we know what we want
and if she doesn't
be willing to figure it out.

We are looking for a woman
that attracts us,
to take ownership,
to be honest, even when the emotions don't fit,
to receive honesty even when emotions don't fit.

Who are more self-aware
then trying to be aware
of what we are not doing,
we are looking for a partnership.

One we can grow
and make decisions with.

Taking full account of each other's strengths
and respecting how we can work in OUR benefit.
We look for the ones that we can struggle with.

The ones that'll call us on our shit
with more facts than feelings
but can love us right through it.

Someone who is willing
to have hard conversations
but knows when to table it.

The ones that speak
and are willing
to learn our love language.

You see the thing about
knowing yourself
is that you get to a place
when you accept
who you've become
and design where you are going
and while everyone may know how to run
it doesn't make them a runner
and every pilot isn't an astronaut.

So, if you're the only one
I'm supposed to spend my life with
there is a training
for each other's hearts
that we must teach.

The time that we spend
must be intentional
just as much as it was an accident.

We must know what we're made of
so that our love can survive
what it's up against.

There's a group of us [men]
that want to love you
in and through a lifetime

and not just for the gram.

•••

Reflections
We're all looking for the same thing! We're just trying to see it in someone else.

Ladies there is nothing wrong with being successful or being able to handle things on your own. The challenge is can you provide the place that a man fits outside of just the title?

Sometimes we don't know where you want us to fit.

Money gets you through life. Relationships get you the most out of it!

•••

Everyone Doesn't Past Go

Women don't date any and everyone
that want to date them.
Why should men?

Just because a woman thinks she's the package
doesn't mean the person or people she wants,
wants to buy it!

You must know how to sell yourself and market you!

•••

Reflections

Whatever we see in ourselves as being valuable doesn't
mean other people will see it. The question becomes, "Did
I develop these attributes for me or for them?"

If for you then everyone will not appreciate it like you do
because you put the work in. If for them, more people will
like it, but it may not be the attention you're looking for.

People cannot deposit beyond what they are already full
of. Give energy accordingly.

•••

Proposed Dating Guidelines

Learn yourself.
Learn what you like and dislike.
Learn the why behind your anxieties and fears.
Face them and heal from them.

Know what you're looking for and willing to accept in any given interaction.
Accept that things change but the core of who you are should not.

Know your categories e.g. just friends, intimate, relationship, marriage, friends with benefits, etc. Know what the characteristics are that make up those categories. Don't make or remix the category to make someone fit that doesn't.

Communicate.
Ask questions to understand where the other person is coming from.
Learn their story.
Be okay with walking away and for them to walk away from you.
Communicate anxieties and know how to listen and process others.

•••

Reflections

Stick to your script. If you know you can't do something outside of the context that you want without catching feelings or without anxiety, DO NOT DO IT!

If the price to pay is at the cost of yourself and you don't want to pay that cost, then do not do it. Let your yes be yes and your no be no!

It's Only Fair

If you can change your mind
about liking a guy,
allow a guy to change his mind
about liking you!

•••

Reflections
We don't like the feeling that someone switched on us.
But accept that it happens. Not to heart or to mind. Just
that it is.

If it gets to the heart as hurt feelings, we have to ask
ourselves, "did we expect or assume too much." If we get
angry, "what did we expect?"

Practicing letting go is a process.

Relationships are a commitment
and commitment is a choice.
It's always your choice.

•••

KNOW WHO YOU'RE DEALING WITH.

Everyone isn't groomed to be what the other side is
expecting them to be.

•••

Intentional

We all weren't groomed for marriage
or taught how to be in functional relationships
or know what one looks like.

We just know we want it.

•••

Reflections
A lot of us are broken. Left to figure out what a
relationship is and our responsibilities in it.

Times are changing. We can no longer use what we
weren't taught as reasons not to move forward.

Rather, they should be the reasons we must be intentional.
Intentional about how we listen. What we say. How we
allow ourselves to feel. What we deposit into our hearts.
Who we give our heart to and who we take it back from.

Life Didn't Come With a Manual

This isn't an absolute fix,
nothing is!

However, a huge piece
I'm referring to has to do with what goes on,
on the inside,
of the relationship for women,
when their expectations are based more on imaginary
things than on reality and then placed on him to live out.

Treating a man as if he has a booklet
on how to do things that a woman doesn't have,
as if he has a cheat code to life.

Know when to allow him
to rest and vent
about how he's been beat up by this world
and the disappointments put on him, etc.

Create that mindset
and the place
that says though we challenge each other
I'm patient in allowing you to adjust.

Everyone is trying to figure out this life.
When someone is finally telling you what they need, it's
not because they are pushing you away. It's because there

is something, they're missing that's making it hard to
connect.

Whatever it is,
they don't need you to agree with it,
they need you to listen,
to understand,
and figure out a way to give it.

When you don't,
they'll find themselves
in a place to get it
from someone else.

Again, this is not absolute.

However, if the person you do life with
can't at least be allowed
to tell you how they are challenged by you negatively, and
you listen
with an open heart and mind,
listening for understanding
versus an entitled heart,
or listening to deny,
you'll never connect.

You do not get understanding by talking,
you get it by asking questions.

•••

Note to the Ladies
Men are just as emotionally damaged as women are. We just don't have the open forums that care about our hurt like women do, to be taken just as seriously.

In a relationship providing the space to learn his story and allowing him to learn yours can give context to the "whys" and give space for challenges. This may not be easy, but it's worth it. Also, understand that everyone doesn't come out the box wanting and willing to share. It takes time.

Reflections
Today's man is different. Groomed differently. Not by father figures or married men groups. We've been shaped by experiences and expectations, just like a lot of women. We both have expectations without the teachings and habits to support them. Sometimes, rather than finding someone that has them, it's better to find someone that wants you enough and is willing to learn you!

If the Shoe Fits

I've learned that
if I'm not ready to develop
into a new person
or the person I'm with
doesn't make me want to develop
into a new person
then I can't tie myself to them.

The new person may be in any category.
At the end, at the start,
I know who I am and what I need
while also knowing there's a lot, I don't know
and am learning.

But I have space to receive it.
To receive
from the person that fits
and not the person
that thinks they fit
or wants to fit.

•••

Reflections
Becoming a better version of yourself just happens when
you're in the right company, not by force but by example.
Their very lifestyle makes you want to be better suited for
them and the relationship.

You can't want a man or any person to open up to you
then shut them down when they do!
Know how to receive what you're asking for.

•••

What Lies Beneath

You can't control how someone responds to trauma.

No matter how secure and self-aware someone is
there will be a time that their insecurities come out. The
challenge and work begins when they do.

The question becomes are you willing to create the space
that draws out, addresses, and helps heal? or will you
consider them broken beyond your threshold and not be a
part of their healing and growth process? Not with the
responsibility of fixing them but with simply being
present.

Growth doesn't happen if there isn't a challenge.
Listen to yourself,
ask yourself the questions that make you uncomfortable.
The ones you don't have the answers to.

What do you like? Really like and don't like?
What are you afraid of and why?

Look at discomfort as a place you find yourself in when
it's time to grow.
It's a training ground.

A lot of our outcomes begin first with how we look at
things. Are we looking from a place of love, insecurity,
etc.?

The place we look at things from will create the through line in which we often see to the end.
Your insecurities do not just affect you.

You do not have to be perfect but know and own when your challenges may create more challenges in your life and relationships.

If you have a two-seater convertible and the passenger seat is full of garbage, you're not going to invite someone in your car.
You have to make space for them.

The same thing is true in our relationships.
We have to remove anything that prevents the people we want from having a space in our lives.

Learn to live in balance and rhythm, not stillness.

Accepting that people don't have to do anything at all.
Being consistent is a luxury.

Though you may get information, the getting to know real people takes time.

In dating know what's for the moment and what's for the long term. Know when you're trying to push something to be and what you ideally want vs. what it actually is.

I learned what it looks like having someone that's into me and someone who isn't.

Give people the opportunity to change their mind like you want the grace if you change yours. Know when you mess up. Apologize and ask for forgiveness.

If the other person abuses your vulnerability that's none of your business. That comes from them. You do not have to allow people to be in your life.

Focusing on what isn't your business causes stress.

- Get to a place where you can get to a peace of mind and maintain it and know how to get back to it if it's lost.
- Learn what it means to be humble and receive grace.
- Know how to give grace.
- Know that everyone isn't going to be a certain way or traveling the same path which is okay. Knowing this makes it easier to focus on those who reciprocate vs. those who don't.

While being single.
Understand and choose for yourself, whether or not being single is a place you're staying in or a place you're passing through.

The luxury of being single is being able to work on developing yourself wholly. Experiencing the world in a way that develops patience and accrues experiences to teach. To be intentional.

The same intentions it takes while being single and becoming better at being single will be the same work it'll take when you're ready to get back into a relationship.

Adjusting.
Adjusting and growing is a lifetime process.

Being single just allows us the opportunity to develop and believe in the foundation that makes us who we really are without influence.

It's difficult to do while in a relationship because you're not just developing for you, you're developing for the goal of the relationship. The vision.

Women often wonder why men would rather be in situations (without titles).

When a man makes it clear what he's there for and what he can give he, 1) gives the woman a chance to leave because it might not fit her and what she wants and 2) he's identified that he understands that the title carries expectations and accountability that he may not be ready for.

This could be because of past hurt and failed relationships, or that he just doesn't want it.

Look at it like this: you may like your job, but it doesn't mean you want to be the manager or the owner.

There are certain things I want with:
a life partner
a fuck partner
a friend.

I define my categories and I'm honest with myself and them. If the person doesn't fit the profile mutually, I don't force it.

•••

Reflections
Every one of us are living out our story from a place. Either it's from how someone treated us or didn't. Living out a narrative that we bought into that may have started from a traumatic place.

The thing is the person across from us doesn't know. The question is, are you willing to share it? If you are and they're not willing to listen, then on to the next.

You can't predict how someone will respond to trauma.

•••

Who Accepts You

Accept that just because you tell someone what you've been through and how you are, doesn't mean they will accept it or you.

THEY DO NOT HAVE TO UNDERSTAND AND YOU DO NOT HAVE TO UNDERSTAND in order for it to be valid, but it needs to be shared.
A lot of times people do not comprehend it either.

Take that expectation that they have to get it and change right at that minute, off of your shoulders. If that expectation isn't met, it'll create deeper problems and disappointment.

My best relationships turned friendships were with women who allowed me space to be my imperfect self and showed me I was enough.

You can get along with as many people as you want and can but... everyone isn't supposed to fit.

Growth is a choice, not a right!

•••

Reflections
Communicating about what hurts us or bothers us can be hard, especially when our communication comes with the

expectations of immediate results, understanding, or validation.

Instead of communicating with the expectation of your partner 'getting you' or agreeing, try shifting your posture.

I like to call it, "just put it on the table." Everything doesn't have to have an immediate action step. Know when it does and when it doesn't.

What Are You Depositing?

How can you say you want to grow as a person
and grow closer to your partner,
but lack the capacity
to deposit their facts
and truth about you.

How can you trust
their compliments
but not their challenges?

Learn how to receive love in reverse.

•••

Reflections

Compliments are opinions without challenge. If we can
accept a compliment from our partner (the person we
chose to be/stay in our lives) we must learn to listen and
receive their challenges. They are the ones that have spent
the most time with us.

We really are only different by how we express or act out
from our past.
We all have some type of PTSD!

•••

COMMUNICATE TO UNDERSTAND.

The place we communicate from matters.
From our ego or our heart.

•••

Broken

Men and women
are raised to learn
how to live apart
from each other
not how to be a part
of each other.

We aren't taught
how to engage
and communicate
with each other.

•••

Reflections

We're all taught everything except how to love each other and how to be a husband or wife or great partner.

We're all figuring it out. And those of us that have it figured out went through a lot and made the hard decisions to figure it out.

The best thing to do at this point is to know yourself and learn the person you want.

What Do You Project?

Our decisions
are a reflection
and projection
of what we believe
our purpose is.

•••

Reflections

Who we accept and keep close is our choice. Thus, making them a projection of who we are and believe ourselves to be.

Posture

Challenge, grace,
and communication
are the only ways
we can get through
the growing process.

Asking questions to understand
not to criticize and challenge.

...

Reflections
There is a difference between asking questions to gain
understanding vs asking questions to challenge and
undermine. It all starts with how we feel.

Being conscious of what place we are listening from.
Anger? Love? Hurt? These places project and produce
different results.

Always know the place you're listening from.

People do not know where you come from or your story.
Manage your expectations.

•••

What You See May Not Be What They See

Just because you see
someone to be in a relationship with,
doesn't mean they want to see themselves
in a relationship.

•••

Reflections
One plus one doesn't always equal two in dating.

Sometimes we fix our hearts and minds on the idea of someone when the reality is that it's not our time or good timing.

The disappointment we experience by putting our hearts in this place would not be as bruising if we had just managed our expectations.

Lessons & Capacity

No one wants to communicate
or talk because it's "different"
or the topics are "awkward"
but everyone wants the results
of what full communication
and vulnerability bring.

Be willing to teach the book
of you to the person who seeks to learn.

We all have our own language
we need to be willing to teach
and have the capacity to learn
what someone else is willing to teach us.

•••

Reflections
You will not and cannot have the results without the
work! You may have built and survived a great life single
but building a new life being inside of a relationship takes
just as much work and compromise.

You can't teach the book of you if you don't know you!
How can you tell someone what you want and need when
you don't even know what it looks like for yourself?

Learn how to listen.
Learn how to ask questions.
Learn how to give grace.

•••

It's Still A Process

Being in a relationship with someone
is a process of constant adjustment,
have patience with it.

Like you would have patience
with anything you wanted
and received
and are working for.

Know how to use your feelings to show emotional
investment
but use your logic to work through the challenges.

•••

Reflections
A lot of times when we want something and see it on the
horizon of looking like what we want, we rush it! Force it,
then accidentally break it.
Let it be and let it become.

You can't talk smart to people
that listen to stupid!

•••

Understanding Without Agreeing

Relationships are magnets
for challenges and misunderstandings.

You can't reach understanding
by attacking
because you don't agree.

You get understanding by asking questions.

By viewing the scenario
from the point of view
of the other person
you don't have to agree
in the end but at least
You can reach an understanding.

What you would do
is not what someone else would do.

•••

Reflections
Be cautious of putting unnecessary pressure and stress on
the relationship based on disagreements founded on
different perspectives and opinions. In these
communication moments we focus more on trying to
convince the other person we are right.

In times of foundational difference, first focus on expressing the differences. Then table it and revisit the situation with a clearer mind. Not rushing resolve if it's not quickly reached. Take time to listen, post conversation, to what the other person was saying.

Two different people from two different lifestyles and realities, forging a path together, intentionally, will not be easy.

Ask yourself: "Am I trying to make them like me?" Misunderstandings occur because two people are looking at an issue from two different lenses.

Are you focused on being right? Are you listening from a place of defensiveness or with a desire to gain clarity?

The truth will come out in the results.

You will never find what you're looking for until you GO looking for it!

•••

Final Thoughts.

Fatherhood

To the fathers, you matter!

Your presence, your encouragement, your discipline, your
grace, your vulnerability, your guidance, your wisdom in
your no's and in your yes's!

Allow yourself to feel that gooey feeling of your child's
love and appreciation. Appreciate that!

You had the honor to get to become a dad and choose
daily to be a father.
You've earned it!

•••

Search & Find

There is a way that the universe responds to YOUR particular make up!

DISCOVER YOUR MAKE UP.

Experiment with how the world responds to it. By experimenting with it, you get over your fear and out of your comfort zone. You must GET OUT of that space to BE-COME who YOU are!

Become comfortable being uncomfortable. Accepting that "being in this space is shaping me. It's my class!" Looking at it as, "It's building me. Not destroying me!"

Be in eternal gratitude for the process of discovering you. Because by that very discovery you get everything that this life has to offer to you. In your language. In love. Not fear.

Discover your MAKE UP!

•••

Excuses are a form of self-manipulation!

•••

Conclusion

People think because I'm single, I avoid relationships. I don't.

I avoid selfishness. Lack of communication. Lack of comprehension. Lack of empathy. Lack of consideration. Lack of understanding beyond their experiences.

I love and value love and connection sooo much that until it's who I want, a relationship just isn't it.

The dating landscape has changed. People and society have evolved. But people aren't changing their idea of relationships. No one is on the same page or knows what their roles are. People grow up and experience life differently and are groomed differently.

People want old school Nokia technology relationships when the world has moved into iPhone technology.

I see a lot of relationships and friendships fall apart because at one point they considered each other, which turned into them only considering themselves. Not knowing or caring how to listen to the other person's heart or hurt. They never even thought to ask!

They stop or never started to communicate to seek understanding, only to challenge by building a case against the person THEY chose to like and love.

Men and women treat relationships like trophies (something to obtain, then feel complete) or feel they "have to" be in one, rather than an experience they GET to experience.

We only project what we accept and believe. The people we keep around reflect who we see ourselves being or becoming.

It starts with you. Change yourself and you change what you project and accept. Not in the matter of objects but characteristics. If there is one thing I've learned and accepted in dating is that everyone isn't going to see in you what you think they should see in you!

Also, what you think is valuable about you may not be valued by them.

The balance is learning to notice the people who do get you. Plus exploring whether they're who you want, beyond their challenges and your fundamental differences. Their challenges and your challenges mixed with the collective fundamental differences are the areas where love, real attraction, and connection shows up because that's where the truth is.

Where the work begins is where Love becomes a choice, not a feeling!

•••

ABOUT THE AUTHOR

Vernon V. Jackson Jr. is an entrepreneur, socialite, and multifaceted artist with talents in visual arts, poetry, spoken word, and dance. Since a child, he has had the rare gift of artistic expression and bringing people together.

His ability to articulate the commonality in the human experience in his writing, along with his ability to produce and host top-notch events has allowed him to work with some of the world's top artists.

As an author, Vernon's main goal is to be a bridge-builder for men and women to find healthy space for dialogue and from that space to find common ground to love and to grow in harmony, fostering healthier relationships.

When Vernon isn't co-running Noble Beauty & Barber, planning events, writing and performing, you can find him in the gym or riding the current love of his life, Geneva, his Harley Davidson.
Vernon lives in Cincinnati, OH.

Book Vernon for your next event.
Email: elamental1@gmail.com
Connect with him online on:
Instagram: @thebest1period and Facebook: @elamental1
www.authorvernonjackson.com

Made in the USA
Monee, IL
24 February 2023

28601198R10059